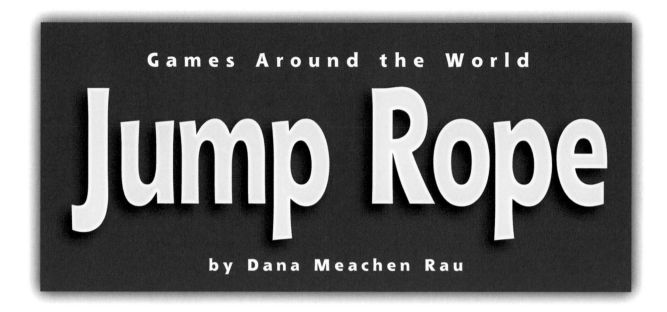

Games Around the World

Jump Rope

by Dana Meachen Rau

Content Adviser: Jean R. Hodges, Vice President, United States Amateur Jump Rope Federation,
and Secretary-General, Amateur Athletic Union Jump Rope Program
Reading Adviser: Rosemary G. Palmer, Ph.D., Department of Literacy,
College of Education, Boise State University

Compass Point Books ✦ Minneapolis, Minnesota

Compass Point Books
151 Good Counsel Drive
P.O. Box 669
Mankato, MN 56002-0669

This book was manufactured with paper containing at least 10 percent post-consumer waste.

Photographs ©: Gary Sundermeyer, cover, 11; Grantpix/Index Stock Imagery, 4; Jim Craigmyle/Corbis, 5; Hulton/Archive by Getty Images, 6; Leonard de Selva/Corbis, 8; Michael S. Yamashita/Corbis, 9; Rubberball Production, 10; Evan Agostini/Getty Images, 22; Frank Staub/Index Stock Imagery, 25; Unicorn Stock Photos/Eric R. Berndt, 26; DigitalVision, 27.

Creative Director: Terri Foley
Managing Editor: Catherine Neitge
Editor: Jennifer VanVoorst
Photo Researcher: Svetlana Zhurkina
Designer/Page production: Bradfordesign, Inc./Jaime Martens
Illustrator: Claudia Wolf
Educational Consultant: Diane Smolinski

Library of Congress Cataloging-in-Publication Data
Rau, Dana Meachen, 1971–
  Jump rope / by Dana Meachen Rau.
    v. cm. — (Games around the world)
  Includes bibliographical references (p.   ) and index.
  Contents: The rhythm of the rope—History of jump rope—Jump rope Basics—Jumping on your own—Jumping with friends—Double Dutch—Chinese jump rope—Competitions—Glossary—Did you know?—Want to know more?
  ISBN 978-0-7565-0677-3 (hardcover)
  ISBN 978-0-7565-1105-0 (paperback)
  1. Rope skipping–Juvenile literature. [1. Rope skipping.] I. Title. II. Series.
GV498.R38 2005
796.2—dc22   2003024094

Visit Compass Point Books on the Internet at *www.compasspointbooks.com*
or e-mail your request to *custserv@compasspointbooks.com*

Table of Contents

NOTE: *In this book, words that are defined in the glossary are in* **bold** *the first time they appear in the text.*

The Rhythm of the Rope

▲ *Jumping rope is a lot like dancing.*

Do you like to listen to music? Do you like to dance? Music has **rhythm,** which makes music good for dancing.

There is a game and sport that has rhythm, too. It's jump rope! The rope makes the "music" with its tap-tap-tapping on the ground. Jumping is like dancing. You move your body to the rhythm of the rope.

Jump rope can be played alone or with friends. It can be played with one rope, or you can play **Double Dutch** and jump with two.

There are hundreds of different jump rope games, and many different names for the sport. Jumping rope is sometimes called skipping rope. Some people just call it jumping. No matter how you play it or what you call it, it's always fun!

◄ *It's fun to jump rope with friends.*

The History of Jump Rope

People have been jumping rope since very long ago. The first jump ropes may have been made from vines or soft branches. Anything long and **pliable** could make a good jump rope. A long piece of straw or grass, a strand of leather or rubber, an animal's reins, or any piece of rope lying about might be picked up by a child and made into a jumping toy.

Jumping rope grew in popularity with the growth of cities. In the 1800s, people from all over the world came to North America to live. Farm families from the countryside moved to larger cities, too. A lot more children lived on one city block than over many miles in the countryside. Jumping rope became a popular city game. Kids could play it in the streets together. Double Dutch, a game using two ropes, was especially popular in cities.

◄ *In the 1800s, jumping rope became a popular game for city children.*

At first, jumping rope was a boys' game. In the late 1800s, though, girls began to be more involved in sporting events. Then parents started to let girls jump rope, too. Girls often wore **bloomers** instead of dresses to make jumping rope easier.

▲ *Girls began jumping rope in the late 1800s.*

Today, boys and girls jump rope on almost every continent. They play many different jump rope games. Kids jump for fun on their own or with friends. Jump rope and Double Dutch teams from many countries also come together to jump in **competitions.**

Children in Iraq enjoy jumping rope. ▶

Jump Rope Basics

How do you jump rope? First you need a rope! Almost any type of rope will do. Some ropes are coated in plastic. Some are strung with plastic beads. Many ropes have handles, which make the rope easier to hold and to turn.

You should also wear good sneakers. You are going to be doing a lot of jumping!

▲ *Don't forget to wear good sneakers!*

Soft handles make the jump rope more comfortable to hold. ▶

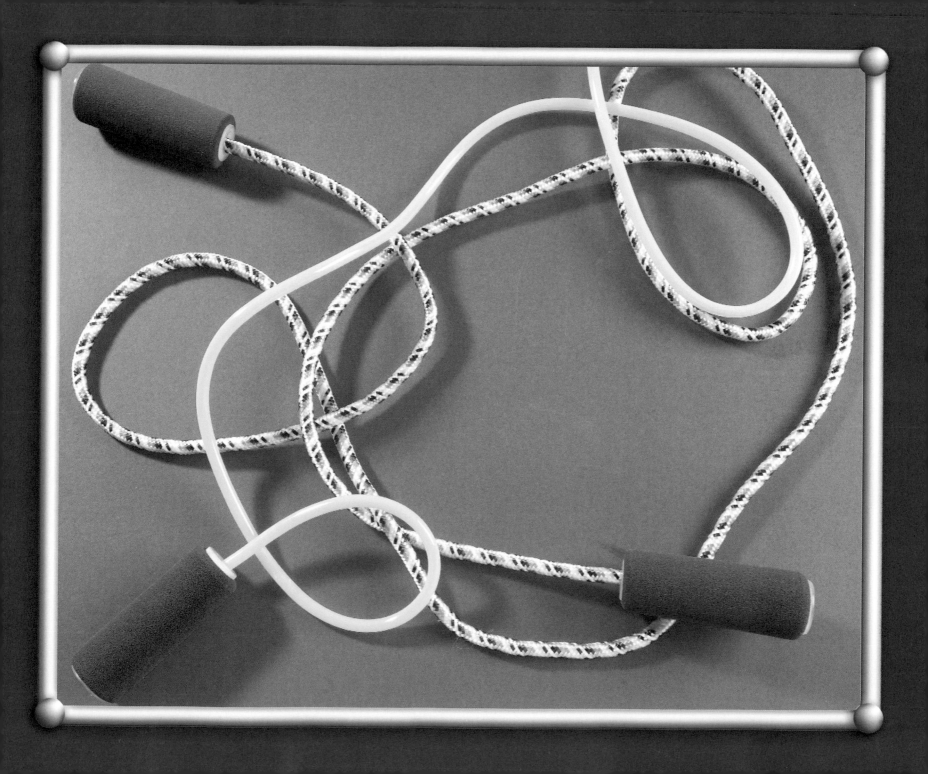

Jumping rope is easier if your rope is the right length. Hold the handles of the rope in each hand. Then stand on the middle of the rope, and pull the ends straight up. If the handles of the rope reach your armpits, the rope is the perfect length.

Stand with your elbows close to your body and your lower arms out to your sides. Don't start jumping yet, though! First you need to practice swinging the rope.

Start with the rope behind your feet. Swing the rope over your head until it lands on the ground in front of you. You swing the rope by making a little circle with your wrists. Step over the rope so that it is behind your feet again.

▲ *Your rope is the right length if the handles reach your armpits when you stand on the middle of the rope.*

Now, without swinging the rope, practice jumping. Stand straight and keep your feet together. Your knees can be a little bent. Take a small jump. You only need to jump high enough to get over the rope.

Now put the swinging and jumping together! It may take a little practice, but soon you will be jumping over the rope on every turn.

▲ *Swing the rope over your head and jump over it as it passes beneath your feet.*

Jumping on Your Own

A few simple skills can make jumping by yourself a little more fun. Try these different ways:

Hopsies

Hop over the rope with only your left foot, or only your right foot, at every turn of the rope.

▲ *Hop over the rope on just one foot.*

Turning

With each turn of the rope, turn your body. Begin by facing forward. Then make a small turn as you jump, and continue turning in the same direction with every jump until you are back where you started.

▲ *Make a small turn with each jump.*

Backward Jumping

Instead of starting with the rope behind your feet, start with the rope in front. Swing the rope over your head and jump over it from behind.

▲ *Start with the rope in front, and jump over it as it passes behind you.*

Crossies

Swing the rope over your head and jump. Then cross your arms and swing. Jump over the rope. Uncross your arms, swing the rope, and jump again.

Hint:

Cross your arms wide, keep them low, and flick your wrists to help the rope go under your feet.

▲ *Cross your arms as you swing the rope.*

15

Jumping with Friends

Jumping rope can be even more fun when you play with friends. Try this game that was first popular in the 1800s. You need one rope and one friend.

Visiting

1. Start jumping with the rope.

2. Your friend faces you. Just after you jump over the rope, your friend quickly steps forward to stand inside the next swing of the rope with you.

3. The next time the rope comes to the ground, you both jump over it.

4. Your friend is "visiting." Jump together for a while.

5. Then your friend turns around so that you are both facing the same way.

6. When the rope comes down, your friend jumps the rope and quickly hops out.

▲ You and your friend are visiting when you face each other and jump together within the swing of one rope.

You can jump rope with two or more friends as well. For games with three or more players, you need a long rope and two people to be **enders.** Enders are the people who turn the rope while others jump. **Hot Pepper** is a popular game for three players.

Hot Pepper

1. While one person jumps in the center, two enders turn the rope slowly and chant the following rhyme:
   Bubble gum, bubble gum, keep the pace.
   How many bubbles popped on your face?
   One, two, three, four, five ...

Rhymes are an important part of jump rope games. People often chant rhymes as they jump to help them keep the beat. Rhymes used for jump rope games come from many countries and from popular childhood poems throughout history.

2. When the enders start counting, they turn the rope as fast as they can. See how many jumps the jumper can make without missing.

3. Switch turns so that the jumper is now an ender. Keep switching until everyone gets a turn to jump. See who can make the most jumps without missing.

▲ *The enders turn the rope as fast as they can while the jumper jumps.*

19

Double Dutch

Once you've practiced playing on your own and then have added a few friends, why not add another rope?

To play Double Dutch you need: two enders, one or more jumpers for the center, and two long ropes, each 12 to 14 feet (3.6 to 4.3 meters) long

Swinging

1. The enders face each other and hold the ends of each rope in each hand. They stretch the ropes out between them so that each makes a straight line.

2. One ender swings his or her right arm in a circle in a counter-clockwise direction and then swings his or her left arm in a circle in a clockwise direction.

3. Then the other ender joins in and makes these small circles, too.

4. The enders move closer together until the ropes brush the floor.

5. The enders keep swinging the rope. Now it is time for a jumper to jump in!

▲ *In Double Dutch, the enders swing two ropes.*

Jumping

The circling ropes create a tunnel shape in the center. With two ropes swinging back and forth, it is hard to get inside. The jumper has to be quick. When one rope is on the ground, the other one is overhead. There is very little time to jump in.

Once the jumper is inside the swinging ropes, he or she turns to face an ender and starts jumping fast! The jumping is more like running in place, with one foot up and then the other.

▲ Kids playing Double Dutch at a street fair in New York City

Chinese Jump Rope

This is a game for three players. Instead of swinging the rope, the ends of the rope are tied together to form a loop. (Instead of using a regular jump rope, you can use a Chinese jump rope that is made of a stretchy material, sort of like a large rubber band.) The two enders stand with the rope around their ankles, forming a rectangular shape with the rope.

▲ *The enders stand with the rope around their ankles.*

1. Start on the outside of the rope.

2. Then jump into the center and say "in."

3. Now **straddle** both sides of the rope and say "out."

4. Then jump and straddle one side of the rope and say "side."

5. Then jump and straddle the other side and say "side."

6. Then jump on both sides of the rope and say "on."

7. Then jump "out" again, straddling both sides of the rope.

8. Next, use one foot to grab the underside of one side of the rope and pull it over the other. Pull at the other side with your other foot until you are standing within a diamond shape. Say "in."

▲ *Pull at the rope with each foot until you are standing inside a diamond shape.*

9. Jump out of the diamond, straddle both ropes as they snap back to their original positions, and say "out."

▲ *A skilled jumper tries to straddle a waist-high rope.*

If you get through all these steps without missing or stepping on the rope, the game gets a little harder. The enders move the rope up to their knees. The next time, they move it up to their waists. The better you do, the higher you have to jump. How high do you think you could go?

Competitions

Some people enjoy jumping rope so much and are so good at it that they compete to see who is the best. Jump rope competitions bring together teams from all over the world. These teams are made mostly of kids, from elementary school through college, but adults jump, too. The teams train very hard. They see who can jump the fastest and who can do the fanciest and most difficult jumps.

▲ *You can jump rope almost anywhere.*

Most kids, though, jump right at home in their neighborhoods, on their school playgrounds, or in their city parks. You just need a rope to play, so get a rope and dance to the rhythm!

◀ *Many kids jumping together is a challenge!*

27

Glossary

bloomers—short, loose-fitting pants worn by women under their skirts in the late 1800s

competitions—organized contests

Double Dutch—a jump rope game played with two ropes

enders—the people turning the ends of the rope; in Chinese jump rope, enders use their bodies to form a rectangular shape with the rope.

Hot Pepper—a jump rope game in which the rope is turned very fast

pliable—easy to bend

rhythm—the repeated beat in music

straddle—to jump or stand so that the rope is between the legs

Did You Know?

 Jumping rope is good exercise for your heart, lungs, and muscles. It can help make you strong and quick.

 Jump Rope for Heart is a popular program in many schools. It is sponsored by the American Heart Association. Kids jump to help raise money for heart research.

 Muhammad Ali, a famous boxer, jumped rope for training exercise. Today, athletes in many different sports also train by jumping rope.

 David Walker, a police officer in New York City's Harlem, is responsible for making Double Dutch the popular game it is today. He helped organize Double Dutch into a competitive sport in the 1970s.

The Amateur Athletic Union (AAU) includes a jump rope event in the AAU Junior Olympic Games every year.

 The U.S. National Jump Rope Championship is held at Walt Disney World each year and is broadcast on television.

 Competitive jump rope teams often have fun names. The Sweet Snazzy Steppers and the Jammin' Jumpers are two.

Want to Know More?

More Books to Read

Boardman, Bob. *Red Hot Peppers: The Skookum Book of Jump Rope Games, Rhymes, and Fancy Footwork.* Seattle: Sasquatch Books, 1993.

Chambers, Veronica. *Double Dutch: A Celebration of Jump Rope, Rhyme, and Sisterhood.* New York: Jump at the Sun/Hyperion Books for Children, 2002.

Dotlich, Rebecca Kai. *Over in the Pink House: New Jump-Rope Rhymes.* Honesdale, Pa.: Boyds Mills Press, 2004.

Scruggs, Afi. *Jump Rope Magic.* New York: Blue Sky Press, 2000.

USA JUMP ROPE. *Jump Rope—A Basic Instructional Guide.* Huntsville, Texas: USAJRF Publications, 2002.

On the Web

For more information on this topic, use FactHound.

1. Go to *www.facthound.com*
2. Type in this book ID: 0756506778
3. Click on the *Fetch It* button.

FactHound will find the best Web sites for you.

On the Road

Strong Museum's National Toy Hall of Fame
1 Manhattan Square
Rochester, NY 14607
585/263-2700
To see a collection of important historical toys, including jump ropes

First-place Double Dutch tournament winners from every state and many countries compete in the World Invitational Tournament. It is held in a different state every year. To find out where the competitions will be, visit the American Double Dutch League's Web site at *www.usaddl.org*

To find out where the next U.S. Amateur Jump Rope Federation (USAJRF) local competitions will be and when the U.S. National Jump Rope Championship will be at Walt Disney World, visit *www.usajrf.org*

Index

About the Author

Dana Meachen Rau is an author, editor, and illustrator.
A graduate of Trinity College in Hartford, Connecticut,
she has written more than 90 books for children, including
nonfiction, biographies, early readers, and historical fiction.
As a child, Ms. Rau and her best friend, Eileen, jumped rope
together all summer long on their dead-end street. Today,
she is teaching her children, Charlie and Allison, how to
jump rope, too. She plays with them, and her husband,
Chris, in Burlington, Connecticut.